60 Chinese Recipes for Home

By: Kelly Johnson

Table of Contents

Recipes

- Beef and Broccoli Stir-Fry
- Sweet and Sour Chicken
- Vegetable Spring Rolls
- Hot and Sour Soup
- Kung Pao Chicken
- Dan Dan Noodles
- Peking Duck Wraps
- General Tso's Chicken
- Shrimp Dumplings (Har Gow)
- Egg Fried Rice
- Mapo Tofu
- Steamed Fish with Ginger and Soy Sauce
- Chinese Scallion Pancakes
- Szechuan Shrimp
- Mongolian Beef
- Chinese Barbecue Pork (Char Siu)
- Egg Drop Soup
- Chinese Braised Pork Belly
- Chinese Eggplant with Garlic Sauce
- Chinese Chicken and Broccoli Stir-Fry
- Chinese Garlic Ginger Shrimp
- Chinese Dry-Fried String Beans
- Chinese Kung Pao Chicken

- Chinese Lemon Chicken
- Chinese Black Bean Chicken
- Chinese Cashew Chicken
- Chinese Sesame Chicken
- Chinese Spicy Garlic Shrimp
- Chinese Honey Walnut Shrimp
- Chinese Five Spice Chicken
- Chinese Chicken Chow Mein
- Chinese Garlic Ginger Bok Choy
- Chinese Ginger Scallion Noodles
- Chinese Broccoli with Oyster Sauce
- Chinese Shrimp and Broccoli Stir-Fry
- Chinese Beef and Broccoli
- Chinese Orange Chicken
- Chinese Black Pepper Beef
- Chinese Garlic Chicken
- Chinese Hoisin Chicken
- Chinese Lemon Garlic Shrimp
- Chinese Five-Spice Chicken
- Chinese Teriyaki Beef
- Chinese Black Bean Garlic Chicken
- Chinese Szechuan Shrimp
- Chinese Sweet and Sour Pork
- Chinese Ginger Beef Stir-Fry
- Chinese Moo Shu Vegetables
- Chinese Garlic Butter Shrimp
- Stir-Fried Snow Peas and Water Chestnuts

- Vegetarian Ma Po Tofu
- Hoisin-Glazed Tofu Stir-Fry
- Garlic Sesame Noodles with Bok Choy
- Vegetarian Chinese Cabbage Dumplings
- Spicy Sichuan Noodles with Peanut Sauce
- Vegetarian Dim Sum: Steamed Vegetable Buns (Baozi)
- Vegetarian Mapo Tofu
- Vegetarian Shanghai-Style Fried Noodles
- Crispy Tofu with Sweet Chili Sauce
- Chinese Sweet Chili Tofu Stir-Fry

Beef and Broccoli Stir-Fry

Ingredients:

- 1 lb (450g) beef sirloin or flank steak, thinly sliced
- 3 cups broccoli florets
- 2 tablespoons vegetable oil
- 3 cloves garlic, minced
- 1 teaspoon fresh ginger, grated
- 1/4 cup soy sauce
- 2 tablespoons oyster sauce
- 1 tablespoon cornstarch (mixed with 2 tablespoons water to make a slurry)
- 1 tablespoon sesame oil
- 2 tablespoons water
- 1 teaspoon sugar
- Sesame seeds and green onions for garnish (optional)

Instructions:

In a bowl, marinate the sliced beef with soy sauce and let it sit for about 15-20 minutes.

In a wok or large skillet, heat vegetable oil over medium-high heat. Add minced garlic and grated ginger, stir-frying for about 30 seconds until fragrant.

Add the marinated beef slices to the wok and stir-fry until browned. Once cooked, remove the beef from the wok and set aside.

In the same wok, add a bit more oil if needed and stir-fry the broccoli florets for about 2-3 minutes until they are bright green and slightly tender.

Return the cooked beef to the wok with the broccoli.

In a small bowl, mix soy sauce, oyster sauce, water, sugar, and the cornstarch slurry.

Pour the sauce mixture over the beef and broccoli. Stir-fry for an additional 2-3 minutes until the sauce thickens and coats the ingredients evenly.

Drizzle sesame oil over the stir-fry and give it a final toss.

Garnish with sesame seeds and chopped green onions if desired.

Serve the Beef and Broccoli Stir-Fry over rice or noodles. Enjoy your delicious Chinese dish!

Sweet and Sour Chicken

Ingredients:

- 1 lb (450g) boneless, skinless chicken breasts, cut into bite-sized pieces
- 1 cup bell peppers (red and green), cut into chunks
- 1 cup pineapple chunks (fresh or canned)
- 1/2 cup onion, cut into chunks
- 1/2 cup carrot, thinly sliced
- 3 tablespoons vegetable oil
- 3 cloves garlic, minced
- 1 teaspoon fresh ginger, grated
- 1/2 cup ketchup
- 1/4 cup rice vinegar
- 1/4 cup soy sauce
- 1/3 cup brown sugar
- 1 tablespoon cornstarch (mixed with 2 tablespoons water to make a slurry)
- Sesame seeds and green onions for garnish (optional)

Instructions:

In a bowl, mix the chicken pieces with soy sauce and let them marinate for about 15-20 minutes.

In a wok or large skillet, heat vegetable oil over medium-high heat. Add minced garlic and grated ginger, stir-frying for about 30 seconds until fragrant.

Add the marinated chicken to the wok and cook until browned on all sides. Once cooked, remove the chicken from the wok and set aside.

In the same wok, add a bit more oil if needed and stir-fry the bell peppers, pineapple chunks, onion, and carrot for about 3-4 minutes until they are slightly tender.

Return the cooked chicken to the wok with the vegetables.

In a small bowl, mix ketchup, rice vinegar, soy sauce, brown sugar, and the cornstarch slurry.

Pour the sauce mixture over the chicken and vegetables. Stir-fry for an additional 2-3 minutes until the sauce thickens and coats the ingredients evenly.

Garnish with sesame seeds and chopped green onions if desired.

Serve the Sweet and Sour Chicken over rice. Enjoy this delightful Chinese dish!

Vegetable Spring Rolls

Ingredients:

For the Filling:

- 2 cups shredded cabbage
- 1 cup shredded carrots
- 1 cup bean sprouts
- 1 cup thinly sliced mushrooms
- 1/2 cup thinly sliced bell peppers (any color)
- 2 tablespoons soy sauce
- 1 tablespoon oyster sauce
- 1 teaspoon sesame oil
- 1 teaspoon grated ginger
- 2 cloves garlic, minced
- 2 tablespoons vegetable oil for stir-frying

For the Spring Rolls:

- Spring roll wrappers (available in the freezer section of most grocery stores)
- 1 egg (beaten, for sealing the rolls)
- Vegetable oil (for frying)

Instructions:

In a wok or large skillet, heat vegetable oil over medium-high heat. Add minced garlic and grated ginger, stir-frying for about 30 seconds until fragrant.

Add shredded cabbage, carrots, bean sprouts, mushrooms, and bell peppers to the wok. Stir-fry for 3-4 minutes until the vegetables are slightly cooked but still crisp.

Add soy sauce, oyster sauce, and sesame oil to the vegetables. Stir well to combine and cook for an additional 2 minutes. Remove the filling from heat and let it cool.

Take a spring roll wrapper and place it in a diamond shape in front of you. Spoon about 2-3 tablespoons of the vegetable filling onto the lower third of the wrapper.

Fold the bottom of the wrapper over the filling, then fold in the sides, and roll it up tightly. Seal the edge with the beaten egg.

Heat vegetable oil in a deep fryer or a large, deep skillet to 350°F (175°C). Fry the spring rolls until they are golden brown and crispy, usually 3-4 minutes.

Remove the spring rolls with a slotted spoon and place them on a paper towel to absorb excess oil.

Serve the Vegetable Spring Rolls with a sweet and sour dipping sauce or your favorite dipping sauce. Enjoy these crispy and tasty appetizers!

Hot and Sour Soup

Ingredients:

- 4 cups chicken or vegetable broth
- 1/2 cup shiitake mushrooms, thinly sliced
- 1/2 cup tofu, cubed
- 1/4 cup bamboo shoots, thinly sliced
- 1/4 cup wood ear mushrooms, soaked and thinly sliced (optional)
- 2 tablespoons soy sauce
- 2 tablespoons rice vinegar
- 1 tablespoon cornstarch (mixed with 2 tablespoons water to make a slurry)
- 1 teaspoon sesame oil
- 1 teaspoon sugar
- 1/2 teaspoon white pepper
- 2 eggs, beaten
- Green onions, finely chopped, for garnish

Instructions:

In a pot, bring the chicken or vegetable broth to a simmer.

Add shiitake mushrooms, tofu, bamboo shoots, and wood ear mushrooms to the pot.

Cook for about 5-7 minutes until the mushrooms are tender.

In a small bowl, mix soy sauce, rice vinegar, cornstarch slurry, sesame oil, sugar, and white pepper.

Pour the sauce mixture into the pot and stir well. Allow the soup to simmer for an additional 3-5 minutes until it thickens slightly.

Slowly drizzle the beaten eggs into the soup while stirring in one direction. This will create silky egg ribbons in the soup.

Taste and adjust the seasoning if needed.

Ladle the hot and sour soup into bowls and garnish with finely chopped green onions.

Serve this Hot and Sour Soup hot and enjoy its delightful flavors!

Kung Pao Chicken

Ingredients:

- 1 lb (450g) boneless, skinless chicken breasts, cut into bite-sized cubes
- 1/2 cup unsalted peanuts
- 1 red bell pepper, diced
- 1 green bell pepper, diced
- 1/2 cup diced onions
- 3 cloves garlic, minced
- 1 teaspoon fresh ginger, grated
- 2 tablespoons vegetable oil
- 2 tablespoons soy sauce
- 1 tablespoon rice vinegar
- 1 tablespoon hoisin sauce
- 1 tablespoon cornstarch (mixed with 2 tablespoons water to make a slurry)
- 1 teaspoon sugar
- 1/2 teaspoon crushed red pepper flakes (adjust for spice level)
- Green onions, chopped, for garnish

Instructions:

In a bowl, marinate the chicken cubes with soy sauce and let them sit for about 15-20 minutes.

In a wok or large skillet, heat vegetable oil over medium-high heat. Add minced garlic and grated ginger, stir-frying for about 30 seconds until fragrant.

Add the marinated chicken to the wok and stir-fry until browned. Once cooked, remove the chicken from the wok and set aside.

In the same wok, add a bit more oil if needed and stir-fry the peanuts, diced bell peppers, and onions for about 2-3 minutes until they are slightly tender.

Return the cooked chicken to the wok with the vegetables and peanuts.

In a small bowl, mix soy sauce, rice vinegar, hoisin sauce, cornstarch slurry, sugar, and crushed red pepper flakes.

Pour the sauce mixture over the chicken, peanuts, and vegetables. Stir-fry for an additional 2-3 minutes until the sauce thickens and coats the ingredients evenly.

Garnish with chopped green onions.

Serve the Kung Pao Chicken over rice or noodles. Enjoy the bold flavors of this classic Chinese dish!

Dan Dan Noodles

Ingredients:

For the Sauce:

- 3 tablespoons soy sauce
- 2 tablespoons Chinese black vinegar (or rice vinegar)
- 1 tablespoon sesame oil
- 1 tablespoon sugar
- 2 teaspoons chili oil (adjust for spice level)
- 2 cloves garlic, minced
- 1 teaspoon fresh ginger, grated

For the Noodles:

- 8 oz (about 225g) Chinese wheat noodles or egg noodles
- 1/2 lb (about 225g) ground pork or chicken
- 2 tablespoons vegetable oil
- 2 green onions, finely chopped
- 1 tablespoon Sichuan peppercorns, toasted and ground (optional)
- Chopped cilantro for garnish (optional)
- Crushed peanuts for garnish (optional)

Instructions:

Cook the noodles according to package instructions. Drain and set aside.

In a bowl, mix together soy sauce, Chinese black vinegar, sesame oil, sugar, chili oil, minced garlic, and grated ginger to make the sauce.

In a wok or large skillet, heat vegetable oil over medium-high heat. Add ground pork or chicken and cook until browned.

Add the chopped green onions and continue to stir-fry for another minute.

Pour the prepared sauce over the meat mixture and stir well. Let it simmer for a couple of minutes.

Add the cooked noodles to the wok and toss them in the sauce until well-coated.

If using Sichuan peppercorns, sprinkle them over the noodles and toss again.

Garnish with chopped cilantro and crushed peanuts if desired.

Serve the Dan Dan Noodles hot. Enjoy the bold and spicy flavors of this classic Sichuan dish!

Peking Duck Wraps

Ingredients:

For the Duck:

- 1 whole duck (about 5-6 lbs)
- 1 tablespoon Chinese five-spice powder
- 1 tablespoon salt
- 4 tablespoons honey
- 2 tablespoons soy sauce
- 2 tablespoons rice vinegar

For Serving:

- Hoisin sauce
- Thin Chinese pancakes (available at Asian grocery stores or make your own)
- Fresh cucumber, julienned
- Green onions, julienned

Instructions:

Preheat your oven to 350°F (175°C).

Rinse the duck inside and out, then pat it dry with paper towels.

In a small bowl, mix together Chinese five-spice powder and salt. Rub this mixture over the entire duck, inside and out.

Place the duck on a roasting rack in a roasting pan. Roast in the preheated oven for about 2 to 2.5 hours or until the skin is crispy and the internal temperature reaches 165°F (74°C).

While the duck is roasting, prepare the glaze. In a small saucepan, combine honey, soy sauce, and rice vinegar. Heat over low heat until well combined.

Brush the duck with the honey glaze every 30 minutes during the roasting process.

Once the duck is done, let it rest for a few minutes before carving.

To serve, spread hoisin sauce on a Chinese pancake, add slices of roasted duck, julienned cucumber, and green onions. Roll it up like a burrito.

Enjoy your homemade Peking Duck Wraps with the rich flavors and textures that make this dish a Chinese culinary classic!

General Tso's Chicken

Ingredients:

For the Chicken:

- 1 lb (450g) boneless, skinless chicken thighs or breasts, cut into bite-sized pieces
- 1 cup cornstarch, for coating
- 2 eggs, beaten
- Vegetable oil, for frying

For the Sauce:

- 1/4 cup soy sauce
- 3 tablespoons hoisin sauce
- 3 tablespoons rice vinegar
- 3 tablespoons chicken broth or water
- 3 tablespoons sugar
- 1 tablespoon cornstarch (mixed with 2 tablespoons water to make a slurry)
- 2 teaspoons sesame oil
- 2 cloves garlic, minced
- 1 teaspoon fresh ginger, grated
- 1/2 teaspoon red pepper flakes (adjust for spice level)

For Garnish:

- Green onions, chopped
- Sesame seeds

Instructions:

In a bowl, coat the chicken pieces with cornstarch, shaking off excess. Dip each piece into beaten eggs, ensuring they are well-coated.

Heat vegetable oil in a wok or deep skillet over medium-high heat. Fry the coated chicken pieces in batches until golden brown and crispy. Remove and place on a paper towel to drain excess oil.

In a separate saucepan, combine soy sauce, hoisin sauce, rice vinegar, chicken broth, sugar, sesame oil, minced garlic, grated ginger, and red pepper flakes. Bring the mixture to a simmer.

Add the cornstarch slurry to the sauce, stirring continuously until it thickens.

Toss the fried chicken pieces in the sauce, coating them evenly.

Garnish with chopped green onions and sesame seeds.

Serve General Tso's Chicken over rice and enjoy the sweet, tangy, and slightly spicy flavors of this classic dish!

Shrimp Dumplings (Har Gow)

Ingredients:

For the Filling:

- 1/2 lb (225g) raw shrimp, peeled and deveined
- 1/4 cup bamboo shoots, finely chopped
- 1/4 cup water chestnuts, finely chopped
- 2 tablespoons cilantro, chopped
- 1 tablespoon soy sauce
- 1 tablespoon rice wine or dry sherry
- 1 teaspoon sesame oil
- 1 teaspoon sugar
- 1/2 teaspoon salt
- 1/4 teaspoon white pepper

For the Wrapper:

- 1 cup wheat starch
- 1/4 cup tapioca starch
- 1 cup boiling water
- 1 tablespoon vegetable oil

Instructions:

For the Filling:

Finely chop the shrimp into small pieces and place them in a bowl.

Add bamboo shoots, water chestnuts, cilantro, soy sauce, rice wine, sesame oil, sugar, salt, and white pepper to the shrimp. Mix well and set aside.

For the Wrapper:

In a large bowl, combine wheat starch and tapioca starch.
Pour boiling water over the starch mixture, stirring continuously until it forms a dough.
Knead the dough until smooth, then add vegetable oil and continue kneading until well combined.

Assembling the Shrimp Dumplings:

Divide the dough into small portions and roll each portion into a ball.
Flatten each ball into a thin disc, creating wrappers for the dumplings.
Place a spoonful of the shrimp filling in the center of each wrapper.
Fold the wrapper in half, sealing the edges to form a half-moon shape.
Pleat the edges, creating a decorative border.

Steaming:

Place the shrimp dumplings on a steamer lined with parchment paper.
Steam for about 8-10 minutes or until the dumplings are cooked and the wrappers become translucent.

Serve the Shrimp Dumplings hot with soy sauce or your favorite dipping sauce. Enjoy the delicate flavors of these classic dim sum treats!

Egg Fried Rice

Ingredients:

- 3 cups cooked jasmine rice (preferably cold and day-old)
- 2 eggs, lightly beaten
- 1 cup mixed vegetables (peas, carrots, corn, and diced bell peppers work well)
- 2 green onions, finely chopped
- 2 tablespoons soy sauce
- 1 tablespoon oyster sauce
- 1 teaspoon sesame oil
- 2 tablespoons vegetable oil
- Salt and pepper to taste

Instructions:

Heat vegetable oil in a large wok or skillet over medium-high heat.

Add the mixed vegetables to the wok and stir-fry for 2-3 minutes until they are slightly tender.

Push the vegetables to one side of the wok and pour the beaten eggs into the other side. Scramble the eggs until cooked through.

Combine the cooked vegetables with the scrambled eggs in the wok.

Add the cold, day-old rice to the wok. Use a spatula to break up any clumps and mix the rice with the vegetables and eggs.

Pour soy sauce, oyster sauce, and sesame oil over the rice. Stir-fry for an additional 3-5 minutes, ensuring that the rice is well-coated with the sauces.

Add chopped green onions to the fried rice and stir well.

Season with salt and pepper to taste. Continue stir-frying until the rice is heated through.

Serve the Egg Fried Rice hot as a flavorful and satisfying dish. Enjoy your homemade Chinese fried rice!

Mapo Tofu

Ingredients:

- 1 block (about 14 oz) firm tofu, cut into small cubes
- 1/2 lb (225g) ground pork or beef
- 2 tablespoons vegetable oil
- 2 tablespoons Sichuan doubanjiang (fermented broad bean paste)
- 1 tablespoon chili bean paste (Toban Djan)
- 1 tablespoon soy sauce
- 1 tablespoon Shaoxing wine (Chinese cooking wine)
- 1 teaspoon sugar
- 1 cup chicken or vegetable broth
- 2 cloves garlic, minced
- 1 teaspoon fresh ginger, grated
- 2 green onions, finely chopped (white and green parts)
- 1 teaspoon Sichuan peppercorns, toasted and ground
- 1 tablespoon cornstarch (mixed with 2 tablespoons water to make a slurry)
- Steamed rice for serving

Instructions:

Heat vegetable oil in a wok or large skillet over medium-high heat.

Add ground pork or beef and cook until browned. Remove excess oil if necessary.

Add minced garlic, grated ginger, Sichuan doubanjiang, and chili bean paste to the wok.

Stir-fry for about 1-2 minutes until fragrant.

Pour in the soy sauce, Shaoxing wine, and sugar. Mix well.

Add the cubed tofu to the wok and gently mix to coat the tofu with the sauce.

Pour in the chicken or vegetable broth and bring the mixture to a simmer. Let it cook for about 5-7 minutes until the tofu absorbs the flavors.

Stir in the cornstarch slurry to thicken the sauce. If needed, adjust the consistency by adding more water or broth.

Sprinkle the ground Sichuan peppercorns and chopped green onions over the Mapo Tofu.

Serve the Mapo Tofu hot over steamed rice. Enjoy the spicy and savory flavors of this iconic Sichuan dish!

Steamed Fish with Ginger and Soy Sauce

Ingredients:

- 1 whole fish (such as sea bass or tilapia), cleaned and scaled
- 3 tablespoons soy sauce
- 2 tablespoons oyster sauce
- 1 tablespoon sesame oil
- 2 tablespoons Shaoxing wine (Chinese cooking wine)
- 3 slices fresh ginger
- 2 green onions, sliced (white and green parts)
- 1 tablespoon vegetable oil
- Fresh cilantro for garnish
- Steamed jasmine rice for serving

Instructions:

Clean and scale the whole fish. Make three diagonal cuts on each side of the fish to allow the flavors to penetrate during steaming.

Place the fish on a heatproof plate that fits inside your steamer.

In a small bowl, mix together soy sauce, oyster sauce, sesame oil, and Shaoxing wine.

Pour the sauce mixture over the fish, making sure to coat it well.

Scatter ginger slices and half of the green onions over the fish.

Fill a steamer with water and bring it to a boil. Once boiling, place the plate with the fish inside the steamer, cover, and steam for about 12-15 minutes or until the fish is cooked through.

While the fish is steaming, heat vegetable oil in a small saucepan until hot.

Pour the hot oil over the fish to enhance the flavors and aromas.

Garnish with the remaining green onions and fresh cilantro.

Serve the Steamed Fish with Ginger and Soy Sauce hot over steamed jasmine rice. Enjoy the light and savory taste of this traditional Chinese dish!

Chinese Scallion Pancakes

Ingredients:

- 2 cups all-purpose flour
- 3/4 cup boiling water
- 1/4 cup cold water
- 1 cup finely chopped scallions (green onions)
- Salt to taste
- Vegetable oil for pan-frying

Instructions:

Place the flour in a large mixing bowl. Gradually add boiling water while stirring with a fork or chopsticks. This will create a rough, shaggy dough.

Add cold water a little at a time until the dough comes together. Knead the dough in the bowl until it forms a smooth ball.

Cover the bowl with a damp cloth and let the dough rest for 30 minutes.

On a floured surface, divide the dough into four equal portions.

Take one portion and roll it into a thin, flat circle (about 8 inches in diameter).

Brush the surface of the dough circle with vegetable oil.

Sprinkle chopped scallions evenly over the oiled surface.

Roll the dough into a log, then coil it into a round dough ball. Flatten the ball into a pancake shape.

Repeat the process for the remaining portions of dough.

Heat a non-stick skillet or frying pan over medium-high heat. Add a bit of vegetable oil.

Cook each pancake for 2-3 minutes on each side until golden brown and crispy.

Remove the pancakes from the pan and place them on paper towels to absorb excess oil.

Serve the Chinese Scallion Pancakes hot, sliced into wedges. You can enjoy them on their own or with a dipping sauce made from soy sauce and a splash of rice vinegar. Enjoy these delightful, crispy pancakes!

Szechuan Shrimp

Ingredients:

- 1 lb (450g) large shrimp, peeled and deveined
- 2 tablespoons vegetable oil
- 3 cloves garlic, minced
- 1 teaspoon fresh ginger, grated
- 1/2 cup diced bell peppers (any color)
- 1/2 cup sliced onions
- 1/4 cup sliced green onions
- 1 tablespoon Szechuan peppercorns, toasted and ground
- 2 tablespoons soy sauce
- 1 tablespoon hoisin sauce
- 1 tablespoon rice vinegar
- 1 tablespoon sugar
- 1 teaspoon red pepper flakes (adjust for spice level)
- Sesame seeds for garnish (optional)
- Cooked white rice for serving

Instructions:

In a bowl, mix the shrimp with soy sauce, hoisin sauce, rice vinegar, and sugar. Let it marinate for about 15-20 minutes.

Heat vegetable oil in a wok or large skillet over medium-high heat.

Add minced garlic and grated ginger to the wok. Stir-fry for about 30 seconds until fragrant.

Add the marinated shrimp to the wok and stir-fry until they are pink and cooked through. Remove the shrimp from the wok and set aside.

In the same wok, add a bit more oil if needed. Stir-fry diced bell peppers and sliced onions for about 2-3 minutes until they are slightly tender.

Return the cooked shrimp to the wok with the vegetables.

Add Szechuan peppercorns and red pepper flakes to the wok. Stir well to coat the shrimp and vegetables.

Garnish with sliced green onions and sesame seeds if desired.

Serve the Szechuan Shrimp over cooked white rice. Enjoy the bold and spicy flavors of this delicious Chinese stir-fry!

Mongolian Beef

Ingredients:

- 1 lb (450g) flank steak, thinly sliced against the grain
- 1/4 cup cornstarch
- 2 tablespoons vegetable oil
- 3 cloves garlic, minced
- 1 teaspoon fresh ginger, grated
- 1/2 cup soy sauce
- 1/2 cup water
- 1/2 cup brown sugar
- 1/2 cup green onions, sliced
- Sesame seeds for garnish (optional)
- Cooked white rice for serving

Instructions:

In a bowl, toss the thinly sliced flank steak with cornstarch until the beef is well coated.
Heat vegetable oil in a wok or large skillet over medium-high heat.
Add the coated beef to the wok and stir-fry until browned and crispy. Remove the beef from the wok and set aside.
In the same wok, add a bit more oil if needed. Stir-fry minced garlic and grated ginger for about 30 seconds until fragrant.
In a separate bowl, mix soy sauce, water, and brown sugar to create the sauce.
Pour the sauce mixture into the wok and bring it to a simmer. Let it cook for a couple of minutes until the sauce thickens.
Return the cooked beef to the wok, tossing it in the sauce until well-coated.

Add sliced green onions to the wok and stir-fry for an additional minute.

Garnish with sesame seeds if desired.

Serve the Mongolian Beef over cooked white rice. Enjoy the savory and sweet flavors of this classic Chinese stir-fry!

Chinese Barbecue Pork (Char Siu)

Ingredients:

- 1 lb (450g) pork shoulder or pork loin, thinly sliced or cut into strips

For the Marinade:

- 3 tablespoons hoisin sauce
- 2 tablespoons soy sauce
- 2 tablespoons honey
- 1 tablespoon Chinese rice wine or dry sherry
- 1 teaspoon five-spice powder
- 2 cloves garlic, minced
- 1 teaspoon ginger, grated
- 1 tablespoon sesame oil
- Red food coloring (optional, for traditional color)

Instructions:

In a bowl, mix together all the marinade ingredients until well combined.

Place the thinly sliced or cut pork in a large ziplock bag or a shallow dish.

Pour the marinade over the pork, making sure each piece is coated. Seal the bag or cover the dish and refrigerate for at least 4 hours or overnight for best results.

Preheat your oven to 375°F (190°C).

Line a baking sheet with aluminum foil and place a wire rack on top.

Arrange the marinated pork slices on the wire rack, leaving space between each piece.

Roast in the preheated oven for about 20-25 minutes, turning the pork halfway through, until the edges are caramelized and the pork is cooked through.

If you prefer a charred finish, broil the pork for an additional 2-3 minutes.

Remove from the oven and let the Char Siu rest for a few minutes before slicing.

Serve the Chinese Barbecue Pork slices over rice, noodles, or in your favorite stir-fry. Enjoy the rich and savory flavors of this classic Chinese dish!

Egg Drop Soup

Ingredients:

- 4 cups chicken or vegetable broth
- 2 eggs, beaten
- 1 tablespoon cornstarch
- 2 tablespoons water
- 1 teaspoon soy sauce
- 1/2 teaspoon sesame oil
- Salt and white pepper to taste
- Green onions, finely chopped, for garnish

Instructions:

In a pot, bring the chicken or vegetable broth to a simmer over medium heat.

In a small bowl, mix cornstarch with water to create a slurry.

Gradually whisk the cornstarch slurry into the simmering broth, stirring continuously until slightly thickened.

In a steady stream, pour the beaten eggs into the soup, stirring gently with a fork or chopsticks to create egg ribbons.

Add soy sauce and sesame oil to the soup. Stir well to combine.

Season the soup with salt and white pepper to taste. Adjust the seasoning according to your preference.

Ladle the Egg Drop Soup into bowls and garnish with finely chopped green onions.

Serve this warm and comforting Egg Drop Soup as a starter or light meal. Enjoy the delicate flavors and silky texture of this classic Chinese soup!

Chinese Braised Pork Belly

Ingredients:

- 1 lb (450g) pork belly, skin on, cut into bite-sized pieces
- 2 tablespoons vegetable oil
- 3 slices ginger
- 2 cloves garlic, minced
- 2 tablespoons Shaoxing wine (Chinese cooking wine)
- 3 tablespoons soy sauce
- 1 tablespoon dark soy sauce
- 2 tablespoons oyster sauce
- 2 tablespoons brown sugar
- 1 cinnamon stick
- 2 star anise
- 2 cups water
- Green onions, chopped, for garnish

Instructions:

Heat vegetable oil in a wok or large pot over medium heat. Add ginger slices and minced garlic, and stir-fry for about 30 seconds until fragrant.

Add the pork belly pieces to the wok and sear until browned on all sides.

Pour in Shaoxing wine, soy sauce, dark soy sauce, oyster sauce, and brown sugar. Stir to coat the pork evenly.

Add the cinnamon stick, star anise, and water to the wok. Bring the mixture to a simmer. Reduce the heat to low, cover the wok, and let it simmer for about 1.5 to 2 hours or until the pork belly is tender and the sauce has thickened.

- Occasionally check and stir the pork during cooking to prevent sticking.
- Once the pork is tender, remove the cinnamon stick and star anise.
- Increase the heat to medium-high and cook uncovered for an additional 10-15 minutes, stirring occasionally, until the sauce thickens and coats the pork.
- Garnish with chopped green onions before serving.

Serve the Chinese Braised Pork Belly over steamed rice or noodles. Enjoy the rich and savory flavors of this classic Chinese dish!

Chinese Eggplant with Garlic Sauce

Ingredients:

- 2 large Chinese eggplants, sliced into bite-sized pieces
- 3 tablespoons vegetable oil
- 4 cloves garlic, minced
- 1 tablespoon ginger, grated
- 2 tablespoons soy sauce
- 1 tablespoon rice vinegar
- 1 tablespoon sugar
- 1 tablespoon cornstarch (mixed with 2 tablespoons water to make a slurry)
- 1 teaspoon sesame oil
- Red pepper flakes or chili oil (optional, for spice)
- Green onions, sliced, for garnish

Instructions:

Heat vegetable oil in a wok or large skillet over medium-high heat.

Add sliced eggplants to the wok and stir-fry for about 5-7 minutes until they are tender and slightly golden.

Push the eggplants to one side of the wok, and add minced garlic and grated ginger to the other side. Stir-fry the garlic and ginger for about 30 seconds until fragrant.

Mix the eggplants with the garlic and ginger.

In a bowl, combine soy sauce, rice vinegar, and sugar. Pour this sauce over the eggplants and stir well.

Pour the cornstarch slurry over the eggplants and continue to stir-fry until the sauce thickens.

Drizzle sesame oil over the dish and toss to coat evenly.

If you like it spicy, add red pepper flakes or chili oil according to your preference.

Garnish with sliced green onions.

Serve the Chinese Eggplant with Garlic Sauce over steamed rice or noodles. Enjoy the savory and aromatic flavors of this delightful vegetarian dish!

Chinese Chicken and Broccoli Stir-Fry

Ingredients:

For the Sauce:

- 1/4 cup soy sauce
- 2 tablespoons oyster sauce
- 1 tablespoon hoisin sauce
- 1 tablespoon cornstarch
- 1 tablespoon water

For the Stir-Fry:

- 1 lb (450g) boneless, skinless chicken breasts, thinly sliced
- 3 cups broccoli florets
- 2 tablespoons vegetable oil
- 3 cloves garlic, minced
- 1 tablespoon ginger, grated
- Cooked white rice for serving
- Sesame seeds and sliced green onions for garnish (optional)

Instructions:

For the Sauce:

In a bowl, whisk together soy sauce, oyster sauce, hoisin sauce, cornstarch, and water. Set aside.

For the Stir-Fry:

Heat vegetable oil in a wok or large skillet over medium-high heat.

Add sliced chicken to the wok and stir-fry until browned and cooked through. Remove the chicken from the wok and set aside.

In the same wok, add a bit more oil if needed. Stir-fry minced garlic and grated ginger for about 30 seconds until fragrant.

Add broccoli florets to the wok and stir-fry for 2-3 minutes until they are slightly tender.

Return the cooked chicken to the wok.

Pour the prepared sauce over the chicken and broccoli. Stir well to coat everything evenly.

Continue to stir-fry for an additional 2-3 minutes until the sauce thickens.

Adjust the seasoning if needed.

Serve the Chinese Chicken and Broccoli Stir-Fry over cooked white rice. Garnish with sesame seeds and sliced green onions if desired. Enjoy this quick and flavorful stir-fry!

Chinese Garlic Ginger Shrimp

Ingredients:

- 1 lb (450g) large shrimp, peeled and deveined
- 3 tablespoons soy sauce
- 1 tablespoon oyster sauce
- 1 tablespoon rice vinegar
- 1 tablespoon honey or brown sugar
- 1 tablespoon sesame oil
- 3 tablespoons vegetable oil
- 4 cloves garlic, minced
- 1 tablespoon ginger, grated
- Red pepper flakes or sliced red chili (optional, for spice)
- Green onions, sliced, for garnish
- Cooked white rice for serving

Instructions:

In a bowl, whisk together soy sauce, oyster sauce, rice vinegar, honey or brown sugar, and sesame oil. Set aside.

Heat vegetable oil in a wok or large skillet over medium-high heat.

Add minced garlic and grated ginger to the wok. Stir-fry for about 30 seconds until fragrant.

Add the peeled and deveined shrimp to the wok. Cook for 2-3 minutes, stirring frequently, until the shrimp turn pink and opaque.

Pour the prepared sauce over the shrimp. Toss to coat the shrimp evenly.

If you like it spicy, add red pepper flakes or sliced red chili according to your preference.

Continue to stir-fry for an additional 1-2 minutes until the sauce thickens slightly. Garnish with sliced green onions.

Serve the Chinese Garlic Ginger Shrimp over cooked white rice. Enjoy the delicious combination of garlic, ginger, and succulent shrimp in this quick and flavorful dish!

Chinese Dry-Fried String Beans

Ingredients:

- 1 lb (450g) fresh green beans, ends trimmed
- 2 tablespoons vegetable oil
- 2 cloves garlic, minced
- 1 tablespoon soy sauce
- 1 teaspoon sugar
- 1/2 teaspoon salt
- 1/4 teaspoon white pepper
- Sesame seeds for garnish (optional)

Instructions:

Rinse the green beans and pat them dry with a kitchen towel. Trim the ends and cut the beans into bite-sized pieces.

Heat vegetable oil in a wok or large skillet over medium-high heat.

Add the green beans to the wok and stir-fry for about 5-7 minutes until they are blistered and slightly wrinkled.

Push the beans to the sides of the wok, creating a well in the center. Add minced garlic to the well and stir-fry for about 30 seconds until fragrant.

Mix the garlic with the green beans.

In a small bowl, mix soy sauce, sugar, salt, and white pepper. Pour this sauce over the green beans and toss to coat evenly.

Continue to stir-fry for an additional 2-3 minutes until the beans are tender-crisp.

Garnish with sesame seeds if desired.

Serve the Chinese Dry-Fried String Beans as a delightful side dish. Enjoy the crispiness and savory flavors of these flavorful green beans!

Chinese Kung Pao Chicken

Ingredients:

For the Marinade:

- 1 lb (450g) boneless, skinless chicken breasts, cut into bite-sized cubes
- 2 tablespoons soy sauce
- 1 tablespoon Shaoxing wine (Chinese cooking wine) or dry sherry
- 1 tablespoon cornstarch

For the Sauce:

- 3 tablespoons soy sauce
- 2 tablespoons rice vinegar
- 1 tablespoon hoisin sauce
- 1 tablespoon sugar
- 1 teaspoon sesame oil

For the Stir-Fry:

- 2 tablespoons vegetable oil
- 3 cloves garlic, minced
- 1 tablespoon fresh ginger, grated
- 1/2 cup unsalted peanuts
- 2 green bell peppers, diced
- 2 red chili peppers, sliced (adjust for spice level)
- Green onions, sliced, for garnish
- Cooked white rice for serving

Instructions:

Marinating the Chicken:

In a bowl, mix chicken cubes with soy sauce, Shaoxing wine (or dry sherry), and cornstarch. Let it marinate for at least 15-20 minutes.

Preparing the Sauce:

In another bowl, whisk together soy sauce, rice vinegar, hoisin sauce, sugar, and sesame oil. Set aside.

Stir-Frying:

Heat vegetable oil in a wok or large skillet over medium-high heat.
Add minced garlic and grated ginger to the wok. Stir-fry for about 30 seconds until fragrant.
Add marinated chicken to the wok. Stir-fry until the chicken is browned and cooked through.
Add peanuts, diced bell peppers, and sliced red chili peppers to the wok. Stir-fry for an additional 2-3 minutes until the vegetables are tender-crisp.
Pour the prepared sauce over the chicken and vegetables. Toss to coat everything evenly.
Continue to stir-fry for an additional 1-2 minutes until the sauce thickens.
Garnish with sliced green onions.

Serve the Chinese Kung Pao Chicken over cooked white rice. Enjoy the spicy and savory flavors of this classic dish!

Chinese Lemon Chicken

Ingredients:

For the Chicken:

- 1 lb (450g) boneless, skinless chicken breasts, cut into bite-sized pieces
- 1 cup cornstarch
- 2 eggs, beaten
- Vegetable oil for frying

For the Lemon Sauce:

- 1/2 cup chicken broth
- 1/4 cup lemon juice
- 1/4 cup sugar
- 2 tablespoons soy sauce
- 1 tablespoon cornstarch
- 1 teaspoon lemon zest

For Garnish:

- Sesame seeds
- Sliced green onions

Instructions:

For the Chicken:

Coat the chicken pieces in cornstarch, shaking off any excess.

Dip each piece into beaten eggs, ensuring they are well-coated.

Heat vegetable oil in a wok or deep skillet over medium-high heat.

Fry the coated chicken pieces in batches until golden brown and crispy. Remove and place on a paper towel to drain excess oil.

For the Lemon Sauce:

In a saucepan, whisk together chicken broth, lemon juice, sugar, soy sauce, cornstarch, and lemon zest.

Bring the mixture to a simmer over medium heat, stirring continuously until the sauce thickens.

Assembling:

In a clean wok or skillet, pour the lemon sauce over the fried chicken pieces.

Toss the chicken in the sauce until well-coated and heated through.

Garnish with sesame seeds and sliced green onions.

Serve the Chinese Lemon Chicken over steamed rice. Enjoy the crispy and citrusy flavors of this delightful dish!

Chinese Black Bean Chicken

Ingredients:

- 1 lb (450g) boneless, skinless chicken breasts, thinly sliced
- 2 tablespoons fermented black beans, rinsed and mashed
- 2 tablespoons vegetable oil
- 2 cloves garlic, minced
- 1 tablespoon ginger, grated
- 1 bell pepper, sliced
- 1 cup snap peas or snow peas, ends trimmed
- 2 tablespoons soy sauce
- 1 tablespoon oyster sauce
- 1 teaspoon sugar
- 1 teaspoon sesame oil
- Green onions, sliced, for garnish
- Cooked white rice for serving

Instructions:

Heat vegetable oil in a wok or large skillet over medium-high heat.

Add minced garlic and grated ginger to the wok. Stir-fry for about 30 seconds until fragrant.

Add thinly sliced chicken to the wok. Stir-fry until the chicken is browned and cooked through.

Add mashed fermented black beans to the wok. Stir well to combine with the chicken.

Add sliced bell pepper and snap peas to the wok. Stir-fry for an additional 2-3 minutes until the vegetables are tender-crisp.

In a small bowl, mix soy sauce, oyster sauce, sugar, and sesame oil. Pour this sauce over the chicken and vegetables. Toss to coat everything evenly.

Continue to stir-fry for an additional 1-2 minutes until the sauce is well distributed. Garnish with sliced green onions.

Serve the Chinese Black Bean Chicken over cooked white rice. Enjoy the savory and aromatic flavors of this delicious stir-fry!

Chinese Cashew Chicken

Ingredients:

- 1 lb (450g) boneless, skinless chicken breasts, cut into bite-sized pieces
- 1 cup unsalted cashews
- 2 tablespoons vegetable oil
- 1 bell pepper, diced
- 1 cup snow peas, ends trimmed
- 2 cloves garlic, minced
- 1 tablespoon fresh ginger, grated
- 2 tablespoons soy sauce
- 1 tablespoon oyster sauce
- 1 teaspoon sugar
- 1 teaspoon sesame oil
- Green onions, sliced, for garnish
- Cooked white rice for serving

Instructions:

In a wok or large skillet, heat vegetable oil over medium-high heat.

Add minced garlic and grated ginger to the wok. Stir-fry for about 30 seconds until fragrant.

Add bite-sized chicken pieces to the wok. Stir-fry until the chicken is browned and cooked through.

Add diced bell pepper and trimmed snow peas to the wok. Stir-fry for an additional 2-3 minutes until the vegetables are tender-crisp.

In a small bowl, mix soy sauce, oyster sauce, sugar, and sesame oil. Pour this sauce over the chicken and vegetables. Toss to coat everything evenly.

Add unsalted cashews to the wok. Stir to combine with the other ingredients.

Continue to stir-fry for an additional 1-2 minutes until the cashews are heated through.

Garnish with sliced green onions.

Serve the Chinese Cashew Chicken over cooked white rice. Enjoy the delightful combination of tender chicken, crunchy cashews, and colorful vegetables in this flavorful stir-fry!

Chinese Sesame Chicken

Ingredients:

For the Chicken:

- 1 lb (450g) boneless, skinless chicken breasts, cut into bite-sized pieces
- 1 cup cornstarch
- 2 eggs, beaten
- Vegetable oil for frying

For the Sauce:

- 1/4 cup soy sauce
- 2 tablespoons hoisin sauce
- 2 tablespoons rice vinegar
- 2 tablespoons honey
- 1 tablespoon sesame oil
- 2 cloves garlic, minced
- 1 teaspoon ginger, grated
- 1 tablespoon cornstarch (mixed with 2 tablespoons water to make a slurry)

For Garnish:

- Sesame seeds
- Sliced green onions

Instructions:

For the Chicken:

Coat the chicken pieces in cornstarch, shaking off any excess.

Dip each piece into beaten eggs, ensuring they are well-coated.

Heat vegetable oil in a wok or deep skillet over medium-high heat.

Fry the coated chicken pieces in batches until golden brown and crispy. Remove and place on a paper towel to drain excess oil.

For the Sauce:

In a saucepan, combine soy sauce, hoisin sauce, rice vinegar, honey, sesame oil, minced garlic, and grated ginger.

Heat the sauce over medium heat. Once it starts to simmer, add the cornstarch slurry, stirring continuously until the sauce thickens.

Assembling:

In a clean wok or skillet, pour the sesame sauce over the fried chicken pieces.

Toss the chicken in the sauce until well-coated and heated through.

Garnish with sesame seeds and sliced green onions.

Serve the Chinese Sesame Chicken over steamed rice. Enjoy the sweet and savory flavors of this classic dish!

Chinese Spicy Garlic Shrimp

Ingredients:

- 1 lb (450g) large shrimp, peeled and deveined
- 3 tablespoons vegetable oil
- 4 cloves garlic, minced
- 1 tablespoon ginger, grated
- 2 teaspoons chili flakes (adjust for spice level)
- 2 tablespoons soy sauce
- 1 tablespoon rice vinegar
- 1 teaspoon sugar
- 1/2 teaspoon sesame oil
- Green onions, sliced, for garnish
- Cooked white rice for serving

Instructions:

Heat vegetable oil in a wok or large skillet over medium-high heat.

Add minced garlic, grated ginger, and chili flakes to the wok. Stir-fry for about 30 seconds until fragrant.

Add peeled and deveined shrimp to the wok. Stir-fry until the shrimp turn pink and opaque.

In a small bowl, mix soy sauce, rice vinegar, sugar, and sesame oil. Pour this sauce over the shrimp.

Toss the shrimp in the sauce until well-coated and heated through.

Adjust the spice level and seasoning according to your preference.

Garnish with sliced green onions.

Serve the Chinese Spicy Garlic Shrimp over cooked white rice. Enjoy the bold and spicy flavors of this quick and delicious shrimp dish!

Chinese Honey Walnut Shrimp

Ingredients:

For the Shrimp:

- 1 lb (450g) large shrimp, peeled and deveined
- 1 cup cornstarch
- 2 eggs, beaten
- Vegetable oil for frying

For the Honey Glaze:

- 1/2 cup mayonnaise
- 2 tablespoons sweetened condensed milk
- 2 tablespoons honey
- 1 tablespoon lemon juice

For Candied Walnuts:

- 1/2 cup walnut halves
- 2 tablespoons sugar
- 1 tablespoon water

Instructions:

For Candied Walnuts:

In a small saucepan, combine walnut halves, sugar, and water. Cook over medium heat, stirring continuously, until the sugar caramelizes and coats the walnuts. Transfer the candied walnuts to a parchment paper-lined tray to cool.

For the Shrimp:

Coat the shrimp in cornstarch, shaking off any excess.

Dip each shrimp into beaten eggs, ensuring they are well-coated.

Heat vegetable oil in a wok or deep skillet over medium-high heat.

Fry the coated shrimp in batches until golden brown and crispy. Remove and place on a paper towel to drain excess oil.

For the Honey Glaze:

In a bowl, whisk together mayonnaise, sweetened condensed milk, honey, and lemon juice to make the honey glaze.

Assembling:

In a clean wok or skillet, toss the fried shrimp in the honey glaze until well-coated.

Serve the honey-glazed shrimp over white rice, and top with candied walnuts.

Enjoy the delightful combination of crispy shrimp, creamy honey glaze, and candied walnuts in this Chinese Honey Walnut Shrimp dish!

Chinese Five Spice Chicken

Ingredients:

- 1 lb (450g) boneless, skinless chicken thighs or breasts, cut into bite-sized pieces
- 2 tablespoons soy sauce

- 1 tablespoon oyster sauce
- 1 tablespoon honey
- 1 teaspoon Chinese five-spice powder
- 2 tablespoons vegetable oil
- 2 cloves garlic, minced
- 1 tablespoon ginger, grated
- Green onions, sliced, for garnish
- Sesame seeds for garnish (optional)
- Cooked white rice for serving

Instructions:

In a bowl, mix soy sauce, oyster sauce, honey, and Chinese five-spice powder. Add the chicken pieces to the marinade and let it marinate for at least 15-20 minutes.

Heat vegetable oil in a wok or large skillet over medium-high heat.

Add minced garlic and grated ginger to the wok. Stir-fry for about 30 seconds until fragrant.

Add the marinated chicken to the wok. Stir-fry until the chicken is browned and cooked through.

Adjust the seasoning if needed.

Garnish with sliced green onions and sesame seeds if desired.

Serve the Chinese Five Spice Chicken over cooked white rice. Enjoy the warm and aromatic flavors of this classic Chinese dish!

Chinese Chicken Chow Mein

Ingredients:

- 8 oz (225g) chow mein noodles or egg noodles
- 1 lb (450g) boneless, skinless chicken breasts, thinly sliced
- 2 tablespoons soy sauce
- 1 tablespoon oyster sauce
- 1 tablespoon hoisin sauce
- 1 teaspoon sesame oil
- 2 tablespoons vegetable oil
- 2 cloves garlic, minced
- 1 tablespoon ginger, grated
- 1 cup sliced mushrooms
- 1 cup shredded cabbage
- 1 carrot, julienned
- 1 bell pepper, sliced
- 2 cups bean sprouts
- 3 green onions, sliced
- Sesame seeds for garnish (optional)

Instructions:

Cook the chow mein noodles or egg noodles according to package instructions. Drain and set aside.

In a bowl, marinate the thinly sliced chicken in soy sauce, oyster sauce, hoisin sauce, and sesame oil. Set aside for at least 15 minutes.

Heat vegetable oil in a wok or large skillet over medium-high heat.

Add minced garlic and grated ginger to the wok. Stir-fry for about 30 seconds until fragrant.

Add the marinated chicken to the wok. Stir-fry until the chicken is browned and cooked through. Remove the chicken from the wok and set aside.

In the same wok, add a bit more oil if needed. Stir-fry mushrooms, shredded cabbage, julienned carrot, and sliced bell pepper for about 3-4 minutes until the vegetables are slightly tender.

Add bean sprouts and cooked chicken back to the wok. Stir-fry for an additional 2 minutes to heat everything through.

Add the cooked chow mein noodles or egg noodles to the wok. Toss everything together until well combined.

Adjust the seasoning if needed.

Garnish with sliced green onions and sesame seeds if desired.

Serve the Chinese Chicken Chow Mein hot. Enjoy the delightful combination of tender chicken, crisp vegetables, and flavorful noodles!

Chinese Garlic Ginger Bok Choy

Ingredients:

- 1 lb (450g) baby bok choy, halved
- 2 tablespoons vegetable oil
- 3 cloves garlic, minced
- 1 tablespoon ginger, grated
- 2 tablespoons soy sauce
- 1 teaspoon sesame oil
- 1 teaspoon sugar
- Red pepper flakes (optional)
- Sesame seeds for garnish (optional)

Instructions:

Rinse the baby bok choy under cold water and pat them dry.

Heat vegetable oil in a wok or large skillet over medium-high heat.

Add minced garlic and grated ginger to the wok. Stir-fry for about 30 seconds until fragrant.

Add the halved baby bok choy to the wok. Stir-fry for 3-4 minutes until the bok choy is tender-crisp.

In a small bowl, mix soy sauce, sesame oil, and sugar. Pour this sauce over the bok choy.

Toss the bok choy in the sauce until well-coated.

Add red pepper flakes if you like some heat.

Continue to stir-fry for an additional 1-2 minutes until the bok choy is well infused with the flavors.

Garnish with sesame seeds if desired.

Serve the Chinese Garlic Ginger Bok Choy as a side dish. Enjoy the fresh and vibrant flavors of this quick and healthy stir-fry!

Chinese Ginger Scallion Noodles

Ingredients:

- 8 oz (225g) Chinese egg noodles or your favorite noodles
- 2 tablespoons vegetable oil
- 3 tablespoons ginger, finely minced
- 1 cup scallions (green onions), thinly sliced
- 2 tablespoons soy sauce
- 1 tablespoon rice vinegar
- 1 teaspoon sesame oil
- 1 teaspoon sugar
- Red pepper flakes (optional)
- Sesame seeds for garnish (optional)

Instructions:

Cook the Chinese egg noodles or your favorite noodles according to package instructions. Drain and set aside.

Heat vegetable oil in a pan over medium-high heat.

Add finely minced ginger to the pan. Stir-fry for about 1-2 minutes until the ginger is fragrant.

Add thinly sliced scallions to the pan. Stir-fry for an additional 1-2 minutes until the scallions are tender.

In a small bowl, mix soy sauce, rice vinegar, sesame oil, and sugar.

Pour the sauce over the ginger and scallions in the pan. Toss to coat everything evenly.

Add the cooked noodles to the pan. Toss the noodles in the ginger and scallion mixture until well combined.

Add red pepper flakes if you like some heat.

Continue to stir-fry for an additional 2-3 minutes until the noodles are heated through.

Garnish with sesame seeds if desired.

Serve the Chinese Ginger Scallion Noodles hot. Enjoy the simplicity and delicious flavors of this quick noodle dish!

Chinese Broccoli with Oyster Sauce

Ingredients:

- 1 lb (450g) Chinese broccoli (gai lan) or regular broccoli, cut into florets
- 2 tablespoons vegetable oil
- 2 cloves garlic, minced
- 2 tablespoons oyster sauce
- 1 tablespoon soy sauce
- 1 teaspoon sugar
- 1 teaspoon sesame oil
- Red pepper flakes (optional)
- Sesame seeds for garnish (optional)

Instructions:

Bring a pot of water to boil. Blanch the broccoli florets for about 2-3 minutes until they are tender-crisp. Drain and set aside.

Heat vegetable oil in a wok or large skillet over medium-high heat.

Add minced garlic to the wok. Stir-fry for about 30 seconds until fragrant.

Add the blanched broccoli to the wok. Stir-fry for 2-3 minutes to coat the broccoli in the garlic-infused oil.

In a small bowl, mix oyster sauce, soy sauce, sugar, and sesame oil.

Pour the sauce over the broccoli in the wok. Toss to coat everything evenly.

Add red pepper flakes if you like some heat.

Continue to stir-fry for an additional 1-2 minutes until the broccoli is well coated in the savory sauce.

Garnish with sesame seeds if desired.

Serve the Chinese Broccoli with Oyster Sauce as a side dish. Enjoy the vibrant colors and delicious flavors of this classic vegetable dish!

Chinese Shrimp and Broccoli Stir-Fry

Ingredients:

- 1 lb (450g) large shrimp, peeled and deveined
- 1 lb (450g) broccoli florets
- 2 tablespoons vegetable oil
- 3 cloves garlic, minced
- 1 tablespoon ginger, grated
- 1/4 cup soy sauce
- 2 tablespoons oyster sauce
- 1 tablespoon rice vinegar
- 1 tablespoon hoisin sauce
- 1 teaspoon sesame oil
- 1 teaspoon sugar
- Red pepper flakes (optional)
- Sesame seeds for garnish (optional)
- Cooked white rice for serving

Instructions:

Blanch the broccoli florets in boiling water for about 2-3 minutes until they are tender-crisp. Drain and set aside.

In a wok or large skillet, heat vegetable oil over medium-high heat.

Add minced garlic and grated ginger to the wok. Stir-fry for about 30 seconds until fragrant.

Add peeled and deveined shrimp to the wok. Stir-fry until the shrimp turn pink and opaque.

In a small bowl, mix soy sauce, oyster sauce, rice vinegar, hoisin sauce, sesame oil, and sugar.

Pour the sauce over the shrimp in the wok. Toss to coat everything evenly.

Add the blanched broccoli to the wok. Toss again to combine all the ingredients.

Add red pepper flakes if you like some heat.

Continue to stir-fry for an additional 1-2 minutes until everything is well coated in the savory sauce.

Garnish with sesame seeds if desired.

Serve the Chinese Shrimp and Broccoli Stir-Fry over cooked white rice. Enjoy the delicious combination of succulent shrimp and crisp broccoli!

Chinese Beef and Broccoli

Ingredients:

- 1 lb (450g) flank steak, thinly sliced
- 2 tablespoons soy sauce
- 1 tablespoon oyster sauce
- 1 tablespoon hoisin sauce
- 1 tablespoon cornstarch
- 2 tablespoons vegetable oil
- 3 cloves garlic, minced
- 1 tablespoon ginger, grated
- 1 lb (450g) broccoli florets
- 1/2 cup beef broth
- 2 tablespoons soy sauce (for the sauce)
- 1 tablespoon oyster sauce (for the sauce)
- 1 teaspoon sugar
- 1 teaspoon sesame oil
- Red pepper flakes (optional)
- Sesame seeds for garnish (optional)
- Cooked white rice for serving

Instructions:

In a bowl, marinate thinly sliced flank steak in soy sauce, oyster sauce, hoisin sauce, and cornstarch. Set aside for at least 15 minutes.

Heat vegetable oil in a wok or large skillet over medium-high heat.

Add minced garlic and grated ginger to the wok. Stir-fry for about 30 seconds until fragrant.

Add marinated beef to the wok. Stir-fry until the beef is browned and cooked through. Remove the beef from the wok and set aside.

In the same wok, add broccoli florets and beef broth. Cover and steam for about 2-3 minutes until the broccoli is tender-crisp.

In a bowl, mix soy sauce, oyster sauce, sugar, and sesame oil to create the sauce.

Pour the sauce into the wok with broccoli. Toss to coat the broccoli in the sauce.

Add the cooked beef back to the wok. Toss everything together until well combined.

Add red pepper flakes if you like some heat.

Garnish with sesame seeds if desired.

Serve the Chinese Beef and Broccoli over cooked white rice. Enjoy the tender beef and crisp broccoli in a flavorful sauce!

Chinese Orange Chicken

Ingredients:

For the Chicken:

- 1 lb (450g) boneless, skinless chicken thighs or breasts, cut into bite-sized pieces
- 1 cup cornstarch
- 2 eggs, beaten
- Vegetable oil for frying

For the Orange Sauce:

- 1/2 cup orange juice (freshly squeezed if possible)
- Zest of one orange
- 1/4 cup soy sauce
- 1/4 cup granulated sugar
- 2 tablespoons rice vinegar
- 1 tablespoon cornstarch (mixed with 2 tablespoons water to make a slurry)
- Sesame seeds for garnish (optional)
- Sliced green onions for garnish (optional)

Instructions:

For the Chicken:

Coat the chicken pieces in cornstarch, shaking off any excess.

Dip each piece into beaten eggs, ensuring they are well-coated.

Heat vegetable oil in a wok or deep skillet over medium-high heat.

Fry the coated chicken pieces in batches until golden brown and crispy. Remove and place on a paper towel to drain excess oil.

For the Orange Sauce:

In a saucepan, combine orange juice, orange zest, soy sauce, granulated sugar, and the cornstarch-water slurry.

Heat the sauce over medium heat. Once it starts to simmer, stir continuously until the sauce thickens.

Assembling:

Toss the fried chicken pieces in the orange sauce until well-coated.

Garnish with sesame seeds and sliced green onions if desired.

Serve the Chinese Orange Chicken over cooked white rice.

Enjoy the crispy chicken with the vibrant and citrusy flavors of this delightful Chinese dish!

Chinese Black Pepper Beef

Ingredients:

- 1 lb (450g) flank steak, thinly sliced
- 2 tablespoons soy sauce
- 1 tablespoon oyster sauce
- 1 tablespoon Shaoxing wine (or dry sherry)
- 1 tablespoon cornstarch
- 2 tablespoons vegetable oil
- 3 cloves garlic, minced
- 1 tablespoon ginger, grated
- 1 bell pepper, thinly sliced
- 1 onion, thinly sliced
- 2 tablespoons black peppercorns, crushed
- 2 tablespoons soy sauce (for the sauce)
- 1 tablespoon oyster sauce (for the sauce)
- 1 tablespoon hoisin sauce
- 1 teaspoon sugar
- Sesame seeds for garnish (optional)
- Sliced green onions for garnish (optional)
- Cooked white rice for serving

Instructions:

In a bowl, marinate thinly sliced flank steak in soy sauce, oyster sauce, Shaoxing wine, and cornstarch. Set aside for at least 15 minutes.

Heat vegetable oil in a wok or large skillet over medium-high heat.

Add minced garlic and grated ginger to the wok. Stir-fry for about 30 seconds until fragrant.

Add marinated beef to the wok. Stir-fry until the beef is browned and cooked through. Remove the beef from the wok and set aside.

In the same wok, add sliced bell pepper and onion. Stir-fry for about 2-3 minutes until the vegetables are tender-crisp.

Add crushed black peppercorns to the wok. Stir to combine with the vegetables.

In a bowl, mix soy sauce, oyster sauce, hoisin sauce, and sugar to create the sauce.

Pour the sauce over the vegetables in the wok. Toss to coat everything evenly.

Add the cooked beef back to the wok. Toss until the beef and vegetables are well coated in the savory black pepper sauce.

Garnish with sesame seeds and sliced green onions if desired.

Serve the Chinese Black Pepper Beef over cooked white rice. Enjoy the savory and peppery flavors of this delicious stir-fry!

Chinese Garlic Chicken

Ingredients:

- 1 lb (450g) boneless, skinless chicken thighs or breasts, cut into bite-sized pieces
- 2 tablespoons soy sauce
- 1 tablespoon oyster sauce
- 1 tablespoon Shaoxing wine (or dry sherry)
- 1 tablespoon cornstarch
- 2 tablespoons vegetable oil
- 6 cloves garlic, minced
- 1 tablespoon ginger, grated
- 1 red bell pepper, thinly sliced
- 1 yellow bell pepper, thinly sliced
- 1 cup broccoli florets
- 2 tablespoons soy sauce (for the sauce)
- 1 tablespoon oyster sauce (for the sauce)
- 1 teaspoon sugar
- 1/2 teaspoon sesame oil
- Sesame seeds for garnish (optional)
- Sliced green onions for garnish (optional)
- Cooked white rice for serving

Instructions:

In a bowl, marinate bite-sized chicken pieces in soy sauce, oyster sauce, Shaoxing wine, and cornstarch. Set aside for at least 15 minutes.

Heat vegetable oil in a wok or large skillet over medium-high heat.

Add minced garlic and grated ginger to the wok. Stir-fry for about 30 seconds until fragrant.

Add marinated chicken to the wok. Stir-fry until the chicken is browned and cooked through. Remove the chicken from the wok and set aside.

In the same wok, add thinly sliced bell peppers and broccoli florets. Stir-fry for about 2-3 minutes until the vegetables are tender-crisp.

In a bowl, mix soy sauce, oyster sauce, sugar, and sesame oil to create the sauce.

Pour the sauce over the vegetables in the wok. Toss to coat everything evenly.

Add the cooked chicken back to the wok. Toss until the chicken and vegetables are well coated in the garlic-infused sauce.

Garnish with sesame seeds and sliced green onions if desired.

Serve the Chinese Garlic Chicken over cooked white rice. Enjoy the aromatic and savory flavors of this tasty stir-fry!

Chinese Hoisin Chicken

Ingredients:

- 1 lb (450g) boneless, skinless chicken thighs or breasts, cut into bite-sized pieces
- 3 tablespoons hoisin sauce
- 2 tablespoons soy sauce
- 1 tablespoon oyster sauce
- 1 tablespoon Shaoxing wine (or dry sherry)
- 1 tablespoon cornstarch
- 2 tablespoons vegetable oil
- 3 cloves garlic, minced
- 1 tablespoon ginger, grated
- 1 red bell pepper, thinly sliced
- 1 yellow bell pepper, thinly sliced
- 1 cup snap peas, ends trimmed
- 2 tablespoons hoisin sauce (for the sauce)
- 1 tablespoon soy sauce (for the sauce)
- 1 teaspoon sugar
- 1/2 teaspoon sesame oil
- Sesame seeds for garnish (optional)
- Sliced green onions for garnish (optional)
- Cooked white rice for serving

Instructions:

In a bowl, marinate bite-sized chicken pieces in hoisin sauce, soy sauce, oyster sauce, Shaoxing wine, and cornstarch. Set aside for at least 15 minutes.

Heat vegetable oil in a wok or large skillet over medium-high heat.

Add minced garlic and grated ginger to the wok. Stir-fry for about 30 seconds until fragrant.

Add marinated chicken to the wok. Stir-fry until the chicken is browned and cooked through. Remove the chicken from the wok and set aside.

In the same wok, add thinly sliced bell peppers and snap peas. Stir-fry for about 2-3 minutes until the vegetables are tender-crisp.

In a bowl, mix hoisin sauce, soy sauce, sugar, and sesame oil to create the sauce.

Pour the sauce over the vegetables in the wok. Toss to coat everything evenly.

Add the cooked chicken back to the wok. Toss until the chicken and vegetables are well coated in the flavorful hoisin sauce.

Garnish with sesame seeds and sliced green onions if desired.

Serve the Chinese Hoisin Chicken over cooked white rice. Enjoy the rich and slightly sweet flavors of this delicious dish!

Chinese Lemon Garlic Shrimp

Ingredients:

- 1 lb (450g) large shrimp, peeled and deveined
- 3 tablespoons soy sauce
- 2 tablespoons honey
- Juice of 2 lemons
- Zest of 1 lemon
- 3 cloves garlic, minced
- 2 tablespoons vegetable oil
- 1 tablespoon cornstarch
- 1 tablespoon water
- Sesame seeds for garnish (optional)
- Sliced green onions for garnish (optional)
- Cooked white rice for serving

Instructions:

In a bowl, combine soy sauce, honey, lemon juice, lemon zest, and minced garlic.

In a separate bowl, mix cornstarch with water to create a slurry.

Heat vegetable oil in a wok or large skillet over medium-high heat.

Add peeled and deveined shrimp to the wok. Stir-fry until the shrimp turn pink and opaque.

Pour the soy sauce mixture over the shrimp in the wok. Toss to coat everything evenly.

Add the cornstarch-water slurry to the wok. Stir continuously until the sauce thickens.

Garnish with sesame seeds and sliced green onions if desired.

Serve the Chinese Lemon Garlic Shrimp over cooked white rice.

Enjoy the succulent shrimp with the vibrant and tangy flavors of this delicious Chinese dish!

Chinese Five-Spice Chicken

Ingredients:

- 1 lb (450g) bone-in, skin-on chicken thighs or drumsticks
- 2 tablespoons soy sauce
- 1 tablespoon hoisin sauce
- 1 tablespoon oyster sauce
- 1 tablespoon Chinese five-spice powder
- 1 tablespoon honey
- 2 tablespoons vegetable oil
- 3 cloves garlic, minced
- 1 tablespoon ginger, grated
- Sesame seeds for garnish (optional)
- Sliced green onions for garnish (optional)
- Cooked white rice for serving

Instructions:

In a bowl, mix soy sauce, hoisin sauce, oyster sauce, Chinese five-spice powder, and honey.

Rub the chicken pieces with the spice mixture, ensuring they are well coated. Let them marinate for at least 30 minutes.

Heat vegetable oil in a wok or large skillet over medium-high heat.

Add minced garlic and grated ginger to the wok. Stir-fry for about 30 seconds until fragrant.

Add the marinated chicken to the wok. Cook until the chicken is browned on all sides.

Pour any remaining marinade over the chicken. Reduce heat to medium-low, cover, and let it simmer for about 20-25 minutes until the chicken is fully cooked and tender.

If desired, uncover and increase the heat to crisp up the skin.

Garnish with sesame seeds and sliced green onions.

Serve the Chinese Five-Spice Chicken over cooked white rice.

Enjoy the aromatic and flavorful profile of this Chinese-inspired dish!

Chinese Teriyaki Beef

Ingredients:

- 1 lb (450g) flank steak, thinly sliced
- 1/2 cup soy sauce
- 1/4 cup mirin (or rice wine)
- 2 tablespoons honey
- 1 tablespoon hoisin sauce
- 1 tablespoon cornstarch
- 2 tablespoons vegetable oil
- 3 cloves garlic, minced
- 1 tablespoon ginger, grated
- 1 broccoli crown, cut into florets
- 2 carrots, julienned
- Sesame seeds for garnish (optional)
- Sliced green onions for garnish (optional)
- Cooked white rice for serving

Instructions:

In a bowl, mix soy sauce, mirin, honey, hoisin sauce, and cornstarch.

In a separate bowl, marinate thinly sliced flank steak in half of the teriyaki sauce. Set aside for at least 15 minutes.

Heat vegetable oil in a wok or large skillet over medium-high heat.

Add minced garlic and grated ginger to the wok. Stir-fry for about 30 seconds until fragrant.

Add marinated beef to the wok. Stir-fry until the beef is browned and cooked through. Remove the beef from the wok and set aside.

In the same wok, add broccoli florets and julienned carrots. Stir-fry for about 2-3 minutes until the vegetables are tender-crisp.

Pour the remaining teriyaki sauce over the vegetables in the wok. Toss to coat everything evenly.

Add the cooked beef back to the wok. Toss until the beef and vegetables are well coated in the flavorful teriyaki sauce.

Garnish with sesame seeds and sliced green onions if desired.

Serve the Chinese Teriyaki Beef over cooked white rice.

Enjoy the savory and sweet flavors of this delicious Chinese-inspired teriyaki beef!

Chinese Black Bean Garlic Chicken

Ingredients:

- 1 lb (450g) boneless, skinless chicken thighs or breasts, cut into bite-sized pieces
- 3 tablespoons fermented black beans, rinsed and mashed
- 2 tablespoons vegetable oil
- 3 tablespoons black bean garlic sauce
- 1 tablespoon soy sauce
- 1 tablespoon oyster sauce
- 1 tablespoon Shaoxing wine (or dry sherry)
- 1 tablespoon cornstarch
- 1 tablespoon water
- 2 bell peppers (any color), diced
- 1 onion, diced
- 3 cloves garlic, minced
- 1 tablespoon ginger, grated
- Sesame seeds for garnish (optional)
- Sliced green onions for garnish (optional)
- Cooked white rice for serving

Instructions:

In a bowl, marinate bite-sized chicken pieces in soy sauce, oyster sauce, Shaoxing wine, cornstarch, and water. Set aside for at least 15 minutes.

Heat vegetable oil in a wok or large skillet over medium-high heat.

Add minced garlic and grated ginger to the wok. Stir-fry for about 30 seconds until fragrant.

Add marinated chicken to the wok. Stir-fry until the chicken is browned and cooked through.

Push the chicken to one side of the wok and add mashed fermented black beans to the other side. Stir-fry for a minute.

Add diced bell peppers and onions to the wok. Stir-fry for an additional 2-3 minutes until the vegetables are tender-crisp.

Combine the black bean garlic sauce with the chicken and vegetables. Toss to coat everything evenly.

Taste and adjust the seasoning if needed.

Garnish with sesame seeds and sliced green onions if desired.

Serve the Chinese Black Bean Garlic Chicken over cooked white rice.

Enjoy the rich and savory flavors of this delicious black bean garlic chicken stir-fry!

Chinese Szechuan Shrimp

Ingredients:

- 1 lb (450g) large shrimp, peeled and deveined
- 2 tablespoons vegetable oil
- 3 tablespoons Szechuan peppercorns, crushed
- 2 tablespoons chili garlic sauce
- 1 tablespoon soy sauce
- 1 tablespoon hoisin sauce
- 1 tablespoon rice vinegar
- 1 tablespoon honey
- 3 cloves garlic, minced
- 1 tablespoon ginger, grated
- 1/2 cup diced bell peppers (any color)
- 1/2 cup sliced red onions
- 2 green onions, sliced (for garnish)
- Sesame seeds for garnish (optional)
- Cooked white rice for serving

Instructions:

In a bowl, mix together chili garlic sauce, soy sauce, hoisin sauce, rice vinegar, and honey. Set aside.

Heat vegetable oil in a wok or large skillet over medium-high heat.

Add crushed Szechuan peppercorns to the oil. Stir-fry for about 1-2 minutes until fragrant.

Add minced garlic and grated ginger to the wok. Stir-fry for another 30 seconds.

Add peeled and deveined shrimp to the wok. Stir-fry until the shrimp turn pink and opaque.

Add diced bell peppers and sliced red onions to the wok. Stir-fry for an additional 2-3 minutes until the vegetables are tender-crisp.

Pour the prepared sauce over the shrimp and vegetables. Toss to coat everything evenly.

Cook for an additional 1-2 minutes until the sauce thickens.

Garnish with sliced green onions and sesame seeds if desired.

Serve the Chinese Szechuan Shrimp over cooked white rice.

Enjoy the bold and spicy flavors of this delicious Szechuan shrimp dish!

Chinese Sweet and Sour Pork

Ingredients:

For the Pork:

- 1 lb (450g) pork loin, cut into bite-sized pieces
- 1 cup cornstarch
- 2 eggs, beaten
- Vegetable oil for frying

For the Sweet and Sour Sauce:

- 1/4 cup ketchup
- 3 tablespoons rice vinegar
- 3 tablespoons honey
- 2 tablespoons soy sauce
- 1 tablespoon cornstarch (mixed with 2 tablespoons water to make a slurry)
- 1 tablespoon vegetable oil
- 1 bell pepper, diced
- 1 onion, diced
- 1 cup pineapple chunks (fresh or canned)
- Sesame seeds for garnish (optional)
- Sliced green onions for garnish (optional)
- Cooked white rice for serving

Instructions:

For the Pork:

Coat pork pieces in cornstarch, shaking off any excess.

Dip each piece into beaten eggs, ensuring they are well-coated.

Heat vegetable oil in a wok or deep skillet over medium-high heat.

Fry the coated pork pieces in batches until golden brown and crispy. Remove and place on a paper towel to drain excess oil.

For the Sweet and Sour Sauce:

In a saucepan, heat vegetable oil over medium heat. Add diced bell peppers and onions. Stir-fry for about 2-3 minutes until tender-crisp.

In a bowl, mix ketchup, rice vinegar, honey, soy sauce, and the cornstarch-water slurry.

Pour the sauce mixture over the vegetables in the saucepan. Stir continuously until the sauce thickens.

Assembling:

Add the fried pork pieces and pineapple chunks to the sauce. Toss until well-coated.

Garnish with sesame seeds and sliced green onions if desired.

Serve the Chinese Sweet and Sour Pork over cooked white rice.

Enjoy the crispy pork with the delightful sweet and sour flavors of this classic Chinese dish!

Chinese Ginger Beef Stir-Fry

Ingredients:

- 1 lb (450g) flank steak, thinly sliced
- 3 tablespoons soy sauce
- 2 tablespoons oyster sauce
- 1 tablespoon Shaoxing wine (or dry sherry)
- 1 tablespoon cornstarch
- 2 tablespoons vegetable oil
- 3 cloves garlic, minced
- 2 tablespoons fresh ginger, julienned
- 1 red bell pepper, thinly sliced
- 1 yellow bell pepper, thinly sliced
- 1 cup broccoli florets
- 2 tablespoons hoisin sauce
- 1 teaspoon sugar
- Sesame seeds for garnish (optional)
- Sliced green onions for garnish (optional)
- Cooked white rice for serving

Instructions:

In a bowl, marinate thinly sliced flank steak in soy sauce, oyster sauce, Shaoxing wine, and cornstarch. Set aside for at least 15 minutes.

Heat vegetable oil in a wok or large skillet over medium-high heat.

Add minced garlic and julienned ginger to the wok. Stir-fry for about 30 seconds until fragrant.

Add marinated beef to the wok. Stir-fry until the beef is browned and cooked through. Remove the beef from the wok and set aside.

In the same wok, add thinly sliced bell peppers and broccoli florets. Stir-fry for about 2-3 minutes until the vegetables are tender-crisp.

In a small bowl, mix hoisin sauce and sugar.

Add the hoisin sauce mixture to the wok with vegetables. Toss to coat everything evenly.

Add the cooked beef back to the wok. Toss until the beef and vegetables are well coated in the savory ginger-infused sauce.

Garnish with sesame seeds and sliced green onions if desired.

Serve the Chinese Ginger Beef Stir-Fry over cooked white rice.

Enjoy the delicious combination of tender beef, crisp vegetables, and aromatic ginger flavors!

Chinese Moo Shu Vegetables

Ingredients:

- 2 tablespoons vegetable oil
- 2 cups shredded cabbage
- 1 cup shredded carrots
- 1 cup sliced mushrooms
- 1 cup sliced bell peppers (any color)
- 1 cup bamboo shoots, sliced
- 3 cloves garlic, minced
- 2 tablespoons soy sauce
- 1 tablespoon hoisin sauce
- 1 teaspoon sesame oil
- 2 green onions, sliced
- Salt and pepper to taste
- Mandarin pancakes (store-bought or homemade) for serving

Instructions:

Heat vegetable oil in a wok or large skillet over medium-high heat.

Add minced garlic to the wok. Stir-fry for about 30 seconds until fragrant.

Add shredded cabbage, shredded carrots, sliced mushrooms, sliced bell peppers, and bamboo shoots to the wok. Stir-fry for 4-5 minutes until the vegetables are tender-crisp.

In a small bowl, mix soy sauce, hoisin sauce, and sesame oil.

Pour the sauce mixture over the vegetables in the wok. Toss to coat everything evenly.

Season with salt and pepper to taste.

Add sliced green onions and stir to combine.

Remove the wok from heat.

Serve the Chinese Moo Shu Vegetables with warm Mandarin pancakes.

To enjoy, spread a little hoisin sauce on a pancake, spoon some of the vegetable mixture onto it, and roll it up like a burrito. Enjoy the delicious and colorful Moo Shu Vegetables!

Chinese Garlic Butter Shrimp

Ingredients:

- 1 lb (450g) large shrimp, peeled and deveined
- 4 tablespoons unsalted butter
- 4 cloves garlic, minced
- 1 tablespoon soy sauce
- 1 tablespoon oyster sauce
- 1 tablespoon honey
- 1 teaspoon sesame oil
- Red pepper flakes (optional, for some heat)
- Fresh cilantro or parsley for garnish
- Cooked white rice for serving

Instructions:

In a bowl, mix soy sauce, oyster sauce, honey, and sesame oil. Set aside.

Heat 2 tablespoons of butter in a large skillet over medium-high heat.

Add minced garlic to the skillet and sauté for about 1-2 minutes until fragrant.

Add the peeled and deveined shrimp to the skillet. Cook for 2-3 minutes on each side until the shrimp turn pink and opaque.

Push the cooked shrimp to one side of the skillet. Add the remaining 2 tablespoons of butter to the empty side.

Pour the sauce mixture over the shrimp and melted butter. Toss everything together until the shrimp are well coated in the garlic butter sauce.

If desired, add a pinch of red pepper flakes for some heat.

Garnish with fresh cilantro or parsley.

Remove the skillet from heat.

Serve the Chinese Garlic Butter Shrimp over cooked white rice.

Enjoy the succulent shrimp in the luscious garlic butter sauce!

Stir-Fried Snow Peas and Water Chestnuts

Ingredients:

- 1 pound snow peas, trimmed
- 1 can (8 ounces) water chestnuts, drained and sliced
- 2 tablespoons vegetable oil
- 2 cloves garlic, minced
- 1 teaspoon fresh ginger, grated
- 2 tablespoons soy sauce
- 1 tablespoon oyster sauce
- 1 teaspoon sesame oil
- Salt and pepper to taste
- Sesame seeds for garnish (optional)

Instructions:

Heat vegetable oil in a wok or large skillet over medium-high heat.

Add minced garlic and grated ginger, stir-frying for about 30 seconds until fragrant.

Add snow peas and water chestnuts to the wok, stirring continuously for 2-3 minutes until the vegetables are tender-crisp.

In a small bowl, mix soy sauce, oyster sauce, and sesame oil.

Pour the sauce over the vegetables in the wok and toss to coat evenly. Cook for an additional 1-2 minutes.

Season with salt and pepper to taste.

Garnish with sesame seeds if desired.

Serve immediately and enjoy your Stir-Fried Snow Peas and Water Chestnuts!

Feel free to adjust the ingredients and quantities according to your preferences. Enjoy your cooking!

Vegetarian Ma Po Tofu

Ingredients:

- 1 block (14 ounces) firm tofu, cubed
- 2 tablespoons vegetable oil
- 2 cloves garlic, minced
- 1 tablespoon fresh ginger, grated
- 2 green onions, finely chopped
- 1/4 cup black bean sauce
- 2 tablespoons soy sauce
- 1 tablespoon chili bean paste (doubanjiang)
- 1 cup vegetable broth
- 1 tablespoon cornstarch mixed with 2 tablespoons water (slurry)
- 1 teaspoon sesame oil
- Fresh cilantro for garnish (optional)

Instructions:

In a wok or large skillet, heat vegetable oil over medium-high heat.

Add minced garlic, grated ginger, and chopped green onions. Stir-fry for about 1 minute until aromatic.

Add cubed tofu to the wok and gently stir-fry to coat the tofu with the aromatics.

In a bowl, mix together black bean sauce, soy sauce, and chili bean paste. Add the sauce mixture to the wok and stir to combine.

Pour in vegetable broth and bring the mixture to a simmer. Allow it to simmer for 5-7 minutes.

Gradually stir in the cornstarch slurry to thicken the sauce. Continue stirring until the sauce reaches the desired consistency.

Drizzle sesame oil over the tofu mixture and stir gently to combine.

Garnish with fresh cilantro if desired.

Serve the Vegetarian Ma Po Tofu over rice and enjoy!

Feel free to adjust the spice level and other ingredients according to your taste preferences. Enjoy your delicious and vegetarian Ma Po Tofu!

Hoisin-Glazed Tofu Stir-Fry

Ingredients:

- 1 block (14 ounces) extra-firm tofu, cubed
- 2 tablespoons hoisin sauce
- 2 tablespoons soy sauce
- 1 tablespoon rice vinegar
- 1 tablespoon sesame oil
- 1 tablespoon vegetable oil
- 2 cloves garlic, minced
- 1 tablespoon fresh ginger, grated
- 1 red bell pepper, thinly sliced
- 1 cup broccoli florets
- 1 carrot, julienned
- 1 cup snap peas, trimmed
- 2 green onions, sliced
- Sesame seeds for garnish (optional)
- Cooked rice for serving

Instructions:

Press the tofu to remove excess water, then cut it into cubes.

In a bowl, whisk together hoisin sauce, soy sauce, rice vinegar, and sesame oil. Set aside.

Heat vegetable oil in a wok or large skillet over medium-high heat.

Add minced garlic and grated ginger, stir-frying for about 30 seconds until fragrant.

Add cubed tofu to the wok and cook until golden brown on all sides.

Add sliced bell pepper, broccoli florets, julienned carrot, and snap peas to the wok.

Stir-fry for an additional 3-4 minutes until the vegetables are tender-crisp.

Pour the hoisin sauce mixture over the tofu and vegetables. Toss to coat evenly.

Cook for an additional 2-3 minutes until the sauce thickens.

Stir in sliced green onions and cook for an additional minute.

Garnish with sesame seeds if desired.

Serve the Hoisin-Glazed Tofu Stir-Fry over cooked rice.

Enjoy your flavorful and wholesome Hoisin-Glazed Tofu Stir-Fry!

Garlic Sesame Noodles with Bok Choy

Ingredients:

- 8 ounces Chinese egg noodles or spaghetti
- 2 tablespoons sesame oil
- 3 cloves garlic, minced
- 1 tablespoon ginger, grated
- 4 baby bok choy, halved
- 2 tablespoons soy sauce
- 1 tablespoon oyster sauce
- 1 tablespoon rice vinegar
- 1 tablespoon honey
- 2 tablespoons green onions, sliced
- Toasted sesame seeds for garnish (optional)

Instructions:

Cook the Chinese egg noodles or spaghetti according to the package instructions. Drain and set aside.

Heat sesame oil in a large skillet or wok over medium-high heat.

Add minced garlic and grated ginger, stir-frying for about 30 seconds until aromatic.

Add halved baby bok choy to the skillet and stir-fry for 2-3 minutes until they start to wilt.

In a small bowl, mix together soy sauce, oyster sauce, rice vinegar, and honey.

Pour the sauce over the bok choy and stir to combine.

Add the cooked noodles to the skillet and toss to coat them evenly with the sauce.

Cook for an additional 2-3 minutes until the noodles are heated through.

Garnish with sliced green onions and toasted sesame seeds if desired.

Serve the Garlic Sesame Noodles with Bok Choy immediately.

Enjoy your delicious and simple Garlic Sesame Noodles with Bok Choy!

Vegetarian Chinese Cabbage Dumplings

Ingredients:

- 2 cups Chinese cabbage, finely chopped
- 1 cup shiitake mushrooms, finely chopped
- 1/2 cup carrots, grated
- 2 cloves garlic, minced
- 1 tablespoon soy sauce
- 1 tablespoon sesame oil
- 1 teaspoon fresh ginger, grated
- 1 package (about 25 sheets) dumpling wrappers
- Water for sealing dumplings
- Vegetable oil for pan-frying
- Soy sauce or dipping sauce of your choice

Instructions:

In a large mixing bowl, combine chopped Chinese cabbage, shiitake mushrooms, grated carrots, minced garlic, soy sauce, sesame oil, and grated ginger. Mix well.

Place a dumpling wrapper on a clean surface and spoon about 1 tablespoon of the vegetable filling into the center.

Moisten the edges of the wrapper with water and fold it in half, sealing the edges to form a half-moon shape. You can crimp the edges for a decorative touch.

Repeat the process until all the filling is used.

Heat a non-stick skillet over medium-high heat and add a small amount of vegetable oil.

Place dumplings in the skillet, ensuring they are not touching. Cook for 2-3 minutes until the bottoms are golden brown.

Pour about 1/4 cup of water into the skillet and cover with a lid. Steam the dumplings for an additional 5-7 minutes until the wrappers are cooked through.

Remove the lid and let the dumplings continue to cook until the water evaporates and the bottoms become crispy again.

Serve the Vegetarian Chinese Cabbage Dumplings with soy sauce or your favorite dipping sauce.

Enjoy these delicious and homemade Vegetarian Chinese Cabbage Dumplings!

Spicy Sichuan Noodles with Peanut Sauce

Ingredients:

- 8 ounces Chinese wheat noodles or soba noodles
- 2 tablespoons sesame oil
- 3 tablespoons soy sauce
- 2 tablespoons black vinegar
- 1 tablespoon sugar
- 2 tablespoons creamy peanut butter
- 1 tablespoon chili oil (adjust to taste)
- 2 cloves garlic, minced
- 1 teaspoon fresh ginger, grated
- 1/2 cup cucumber, julienned
- 1/4 cup green onions, sliced
- 2 tablespoons roasted peanuts, chopped
- Fresh cilantro for garnish (optional)

Instructions:

Cook the Chinese wheat noodles or soba noodles according to the package instructions. Drain and set aside.

In a bowl, whisk together sesame oil, soy sauce, black vinegar, sugar, peanut butter, chili oil, minced garlic, and grated ginger to make the sauce.

Pour the sauce over the cooked noodles and toss to coat them evenly.

Add julienned cucumber and sliced green onions to the noodles. Toss to combine.

Garnish with chopped roasted peanuts and fresh cilantro if desired.

Serve the Spicy Sichuan Noodles with Peanut Sauce immediately.

Enjoy the bold flavors of these Spicy Sichuan Noodles with Peanut Sauce!

Vegetarian Dim Sum: Steamed Vegetable Buns (Baozi)

Ingredients:

For the Dough:

- 2 cups all-purpose flour
- 1 teaspoon active dry yeast
- 1 teaspoon sugar
- 3/4 cup warm water

For the Filling:

- 1 cup cabbage, finely shredded
- 1 carrot, grated
- 1/2 cup shiitake mushrooms, finely chopped
- 1/4 cup bamboo shoots, finely chopped
- 2 tablespoons soy sauce
- 1 tablespoon sesame oil
- 1 teaspoon sugar
- 1 teaspoon fresh ginger, grated

Instructions:

For the Dough:

In a bowl, combine warm water, sugar, and active dry yeast. Let it sit for 5-10 minutes until it becomes frothy.

In a large mixing bowl, gradually add the yeast mixture to the flour, stirring continuously.

Knead the dough until it becomes smooth and elastic. Cover the bowl with a damp cloth and let it rise in a warm place for about 1 hour or until doubled in size.

For the Filling:

In a pan, heat sesame oil over medium heat. Add grated ginger and stir for about 30 seconds.

Add shredded cabbage, grated carrot, chopped shiitake mushrooms, and bamboo shoots. Stir-fry for 3-5 minutes until the vegetables are tender.

Add soy sauce and sugar to the vegetable mixture. Stir well and cook for an additional 2 minutes. Remove from heat and let it cool.

Assembling and Steaming:

Punch down the risen dough and divide it into small balls.

Roll each ball into a flat circle, making the edges thinner than the center.

Spoon a portion of the vegetable filling into the center of each dough circle.

Pleat the edges of the dough to encase the filling and create a sealed bun.

Place each bun on a small square of parchment paper and arrange them in a steamer basket.

Steam the buns for 15-20 minutes until they become puffy and cooked through.

Serve the Steamed Vegetable Buns hot, and enjoy your vegetarian dim sum!

These Steamed Vegetable Buns make for a delightful and wholesome dish!

Vegetarian Mapo Tofu

Ingredients:

- 1 block (14 ounces) firm tofu, cubed
- 2 tablespoons vegetable oil
- 2 cloves garlic, minced
- 1 tablespoon fresh ginger, grated
- 2 tablespoons doubanjiang (spicy bean paste)
- 1 tablespoon soy sauce
- 1 tablespoon fermented black beans, rinsed and chopped
- 1 teaspoon Sichuan peppercorns, toasted and ground
- 1 cup vegetable broth
- 2 tablespoons cornstarch mixed with 3 tablespoons water (slurry)
- 2 green onions, sliced
- 1 teaspoon sesame oil

Instructions:

Heat vegetable oil in a wok or large skillet over medium-high heat.

Add minced garlic and grated ginger, stir-frying for about 30 seconds until fragrant.

Add doubanjiang (spicy bean paste), soy sauce, fermented black beans, and ground Sichuan peppercorns to the wok. Stir to combine.

Add cubed tofu to the wok and gently toss to coat it with the spicy mixture.

Pour in vegetable broth and bring the mixture to a simmer. Allow it to simmer for 5-7 minutes.

Gradually stir in the cornstarch slurry to thicken the sauce. Continue stirring until the sauce reaches the desired consistency.

Add sliced green onions and sesame oil to the wok. Stir gently to combine.

Serve the Vegetarian Mapo Tofu over rice or noodles.

Enjoy the bold and flavorful taste of this Vegetarian Mapo Tofu!

Vegetarian Shanghai-Style Fried Noodles

Ingredients:

- 8 ounces Shanghai-style noodles or thin egg noodles
- 2 tablespoons vegetable oil
- 2 cloves garlic, minced
- 1 cup shiitake mushrooms, sliced
- 1 cup cabbage, thinly shredded
- 1 carrot, julienned
- 1/2 cup snow peas, trimmed
- 2 tablespoons soy sauce
- 1 tablespoon oyster sauce (vegetarian oyster sauce for a vegetarian version)
- 1 teaspoon sugar
- 1/2 teaspoon white pepper
- 2 green onions, sliced
- Sesame seeds for garnish (optional)

Instructions:

Cook the Shanghai-style noodles or thin egg noodles according to the package instructions. Drain and set aside.

Heat vegetable oil in a wok or large skillet over medium-high heat.

Add minced garlic and sliced shiitake mushrooms. Stir-fry for about 2 minutes until the mushrooms are tender.

Add thinly shredded cabbage, julienned carrot, and trimmed snow peas to the wok.

Stir-fry for an additional 3-4 minutes until the vegetables are tender-crisp.

In a small bowl, mix together soy sauce, oyster sauce, sugar, and white pepper.

Add the cooked noodles to the wok and pour the sauce over them. Toss to coat the noodles and vegetables evenly.

Cook for an additional 2-3 minutes until everything is heated through.

Stir in sliced green onions and garnish with sesame seeds if desired.

Serve the Vegetarian Shanghai-Style Fried Noodles hot.

Enjoy these delightful and savory Shanghai-style fried noodles!

Crispy Tofu with Sweet Chili Sauce

Ingredients:

For the Crispy Tofu:

- 1 block (14 ounces) extra-firm tofu, cubed
- 2 tablespoons cornstarch
- 1/2 teaspoon salt
- 1/4 teaspoon black pepper
- 2 tablespoons vegetable oil

For the Sweet Chili Sauce:

- 3 tablespoons sweet chili sauce
- 1 tablespoon soy sauce
- 1 tablespoon rice vinegar
- 1 tablespoon honey
- 1 teaspoon sesame oil
- Sesame seeds and sliced green onions for garnish (optional)

Instructions:

For the Crispy Tofu:

In a bowl, toss cubed tofu with cornstarch, salt, and black pepper until the tofu is coated.
Heat vegetable oil in a non-stick skillet over medium-high heat.
Add the coated tofu cubes to the skillet and cook until all sides are golden brown and crispy.
Remove the crispy tofu from the skillet and place it on a paper towel to absorb excess oil.

For the Sweet Chili Sauce:

In a small saucepan, combine sweet chili sauce, soy sauce, rice vinegar, honey, and sesame oil.

Heat the sauce over medium heat, stirring continuously until it simmers and thickens slightly.

Assembling:

Pour the sweet chili sauce over the crispy tofu and toss to coat evenly.

Garnish with sesame seeds and sliced green onions if desired.

Serve the Crispy Tofu with Sweet Chili Sauce as an appetizer or over rice for a delicious main dish. Enjoy!

Chinese Sweet Chili Tofu Stir-Fry

Ingredients:

- 1 block firm tofu, pressed and cubed
- 3 tablespoons soy sauce
- 2 tablespoons sweet chili sauce
- 1 tablespoon rice vinegar
- 1 tablespoon cornstarch
- 2 tablespoons vegetable oil
- 1 red bell pepper, sliced
- 1 yellow bell pepper, sliced
- 1 cup snap peas, ends trimmed
- 3 green onions, chopped
- Sesame seeds (for garnish)

Instructions:

In a bowl, combine soy sauce, sweet chili sauce, rice vinegar, and cornstarch. Add cubed tofu, toss gently to coat, and let it marinate for about 15-20 minutes.

Heat vegetable oil in a wok or skillet over medium-high heat. Add the marinated tofu and stir-fry until golden brown. Remove tofu from the pan and set aside.

In the same pan, add a bit more oil if needed. Add sliced bell peppers and snap peas, stir-frying until they are slightly tender but still crisp.

Add the cooked tofu back into the pan, tossing to combine it with the vegetables.

Pour the remaining marinade over the tofu and vegetables. Stir well and let it cook for an additional 2-3 minutes.

Garnish with chopped green onions and sesame seeds.

Serve the Chinese Sweet Chili Tofu Stir-Fry over rice or noodles. Enjoy the sweet and savory flavors of this colorful and nutritious dish!

Feel free to adjust the ingredients and quantities based on your preferences. If you have any other specific requests or if you'd like another recipe, let me know!

www.ingramcontent.com/pod-product-compliance
Lightning Source LLC
LaVergne TN
LVHW081553060526
838201LV00054B/1882